P9-DHP-880

Dino Nightmare

Julian Thomlinson

Series Editors:
Rob Waring and Sue Leather
Series Story Consultant: Julian Thomlinson
Story Editor: Sue Leather

NATIONAL
GEOGRAPHIC
LEARNING | CENGAGE
Learning·

Australia • Brazil • Japan • Korea • Mexico • Singapore • Spain • United Kingdom • United States

Page Turners Reading Library

Dino Nightmare

Julian Thomlinson

Publisher: Andrew Robinson

Executive Editor: Sean Bermingham

Editorial Assistant: Dylan Mitchell

Director of Global Marketing:
Ian Martin

Senior Content Project Manager:
Tan Jin Hock

Manufacturing Planner:
Mary Beth Hennebury

Contributors:
Vessela Gasper, Jessie Chew

Layout Design and Illustrations:
Redbean Design Pte Ltd

Cover Illustration: Eric Foenander

Photo Credits:
44 Eugene Ivanov/Shutterstock

ISBN-13: 978-1-4240-4652-2

ISBN-10: 1-4240-4652-1

National Geographic Learning
20 Channel Center Street
Boston, Massachusetts 02210
USA

Cengage Learning is a leading provider of customized learning solutions with office locations around the globe, including Singapore, the United Kingdom, Australia, Mexico, Brazil, and Japan. Locate your local office at:
international.cengage.com/region

Cengage Learning products are represented in Canada by Nelson Education, Ltd.

Visit National Geographic Learning online at
NGL.Cengage.com

Visit our corporate website at
www.cengage.com

Printed in the United States of America
1 2 3 4 5 6 7 – 18 17 16 15 14

Contents

Travel back
to the year
8,000,000 B.C.

TimeTours

People in the story

Roy Nagy
a very successful
businessman

Maggie Nagy
a Chinese-American woman,
married to Roy

George Jacobs
a middle-aged man who
works for TimeTours

Celia Perez
a young woman who has just
left school

Dylan Byrd
a young Australian scientist

This story is set in the year 2738, when a group of tourists travel
back in time to the world of dinosaurs—68,000,000 B.C.

Chapter 1

The big bang

Maggie sat in the waiting room at Timeport 10 and listened to her husband shouting. Roy Nagy was one of these men who was good at many things, but Maggie thought he was maybe better at shouting than anything else. It wasn't surprising—he did practice a lot—and now he was at the information desk practicing with the man from TimeTours. Maggie understood why he was angry. She was hot and tired and wanted to go home, too. But even more than that she wanted her husband to sit down and be quiet. The rest of the hall was empty except for the TimeTours people and a few other tourists: Celia and her boyfriend Harvey, and some people from another trip Maggie didn't know. They were all watching Roy. It was just after 10 a.m., on June 17, in the year 68,000,000 B.C.

"What do you mean, another three hours?" Roy was shouting.

"We're very sorry, sir," said the TimeTours man. His jacket said his name was Jacobs. "As I've tried to explain, there's a problem in the power room. Our best people are working on it, sir. We really are doing our best. If you could just take a seat . . ."

"Your best isn't good enough, Jacobs. We've been here three hours, sitting in . . . ," Roy checked his Com, the small computer that everybody carried, "36-degree heat. What's going on?"

"As I said, it's the power room."

Roy hit the desk in front of him and was about to walk away, but turned back at the last minute.

"This company is a joke, Jacobs. This whole tour has been a joke. You know, we paid millions of dollars to come here. We paid millions of dollars to see dinosaurs. You know, *Tyrannosaurs*? *Velociraptors*? *Real* dinosaurs. What did we get?"

Roy pointed at a large TV on the wall showing a Triceratops quietly eating a plant.

"These things. Big cows! The only place I want to see cows, Jacobs, big or not, is in a steak restaurant."

"I'm sorry, sir," Jacobs said, his face going red. "I'll tell the management."

"Don't worry," said Roy, walking away. "I'll tell them myself."

He sat down next to Maggie. Celia caught Maggie's eye and smiled. It made Maggie feel a little better, but not much.

"What a joke," Roy said. "This tour cost over ten million and they can't even get us home. You know what I'm going to do? I'm going to . . ."

"Roy, would you . . ." Maggie began.

"What?" he said. Maggie wanted to tell him to be quiet, but it probably wasn't a good time.

"Would you . . . like a cup of coffee?" she asked.

"Sure," he said. "Coffee. Good idea."

Maggie got up and went to the coffee machine, but its power was off as well. Roy was right, Maggie thought. TimeTours really wasn't very good. Time holidays were only a few years old, and nobody expected them to be perfect. Still, it didn't seem right, Maggie thought. Ten million dollars for a week's holiday and the coffee machines didn't work, they didn't get you home on time, and . . .

Somebody was shouting and running toward them from the other end of the hall. Behind him another man came out of a door, closed it behind him, and hit a switch. Red lights went on and off all around them, and the noise was so loud it hurt her ears. Roy was on his feet, but everybody else was just sitting there.

"Run," the man shouted. "Run for your lives! The power room is on fire!" Black smoke came out the door behind him. Roy was pulling at her arm.

"You two," Roy shouted at Celia and Harvey, who were sitting with their mouths open. "Come with me if you want to live!"

Maggie ran with her husband out the front doors. Dylan, a young Australian scientist from their tour group, was sitting on the grass.

"What's going on?" he said.

"Run!" Roy shouted, taking him by the shirt and pulling him to his feet. "This way—into the jungle."

They ran as fast as they could into the trees. Maggie looked back and saw Celia coming out the front with one of the engineers. The world went white as the Timeport turned into a great ball of fire.

Chapter 2

Adventure

When Maggie woke up the first thing she saw was her husband. Roy's face was black with smoke and there was fear in his eyes. Around them everything was burning.

"Can you move?" he asked her. She tried to sit up. Her head felt light and there was a bad taste in her mouth. The smoke made it hard to breathe and her eyes ran with water.

"Maggie?" Roy said.

"It's all right," she said. "I'm all right. What happened?"

"The Timeport," said Roy, helping her to her feet. "It's bad. Really bad. Everyone inside . . . they're all gone, Maggie."

"Gone?" They were gone all right. The whole Timeport building was on fire. The heat was amazing: nobody could still be alive inside it.

"Have you checked for the others? Maybe inside some people are . . ."

"Celia and Dylan are OK. The rest of them . . . No," Roy said.

"Wow, Maggie, you're OK!" Celia said from behind her. "That's so great!"

"Celia, I'm so happy you're all right," said Maggie, then noticed her boyfriend Harvey wasn't with her. "Where's Harvey?"

"Oh, he's still inside," Celia said. "I guess he's . . ."

"Oh, Celia, dear," Maggie said, taking her hand. "I'm so sorry."

"That's OK," Celia said. "We weren't really so happy together anyway."

"I . . . I see," Maggie said.

"I'm sorry," someone was saying. "I'm so sorry about this." It was Jacobs, the man from TimeTours.

"You'll pay for this," Roy said.

"It's terrible," Jacobs went on. "TimeTours will of course . . ."

"There'll be time for that later, Jacobs," Roy said. "Right now we've got to get out of here. This way."

Holding Maggie by the arm, Roy started into the jungle. Celia, Jacobs, and Dylan followed behind. After some time, Jacobs spoke.

"Can we slow down?" Jacobs asked. "I can't go that fast."

"Maggie, can you walk on your own?" Roy asked her.

"Sure," said Maggie. Roy let go of her arm and put his arm around Jacobs.

"Don't worry, Jacobs," Roy said to him. "I got you, even if your company did kill half our tour group."

Maggie realized that it wasn't fear in her husband's eyes. It was excitement. Now that things were dangerous, Roy was enjoying himself.

They walked through the jungle for several hours. At first Maggie was worried they might meet something dangerous. She remembered someone saying the dinosaurs couldn't come close to the Timeport.

The building was protected by "Boomers"—machines that made a noise dinosaurs didn't like. On their tour they carried smaller Boomers to keep the dinosaurs away from them. Maggie wished they had some now.

"Where are we going?" Celia asked Roy.

"There's a storehouse up here," Roy told her. "That's right, isn't it, Jacobs?"

"It is, yes," Jacobs said. "But the things inside are the company's. I'm afraid we can't just . . ."

"Quiet, Jacobs," said Roy.

It wasn't long before they came to the storehouse, and Roy waited while Jacobs opened it for them. Inside there was food and equipment, even some small Boomers they could carry with them. A large Com stood against one wall.

"Look at this," Roy said, putting things into a bag. "We can live for months with what's in here."

"That's great," Dylan said, "but shouldn't we call for help?"

"Just what I'm doing," Roy said, hitting the power switch on the Com. A TimeTours woman appeared. She was coming from the computer, but it was just like she was standing in the room with them.

"Welcome to the TimeTours Com," the woman said. "Please choose: information, services, or help."

"Help," Roy said.

"I'm sorry, I didn't understand. Please speak more clearly."

"Help," Roy said, more loudly.

"I'm sorry, please say your choice again more clearly."

"Help, HELP," Roy shouted.

"Help," Jacobs said.

"You have chosen 'help,'" the voice said. "Is that right? Please choose 'yes' or 'no.'"

"Yes," Jacobs said. Roy's face went red.

"I'm sorry, I'm having difficulties," the woman's voice said.

"I knew it!" Roy said.

"Please choose: information, services, or help."

"Information," Jacobs replied.

"I'm sorry, I'm having . . ."

"What a joke," Roy shouted. Jacobs kept trying, but they couldn't get the Com to work.

"We need another plan," Roy said. Celia found a map and they talked about what to do. Jacobs wanted to wait where they were. He was sure TimeTours would send help soon. Roy didn't want to wait—he wanted to try to get to Timeport 11, which was about 20 kilometers away. Maggie thought they should wait, but she kept quiet.

"I'm not staying here and waiting for TimeTours," Roy was saying. "We'll be here for the rest of the year."

"It will be dangerous," Jacobs said. "There may well be big dinosaurs, even Tyrannosaurs."

Maggie *really* wished he hadn't said that. Roy smiled.

"Are you scared, Jacobs?" he asked.

"Well, yes," Jacobs replied.

"Listen, people," Roy began. "Dinosaurs may be big and they may be dangerous. But there's one thing we have that they don't have. Do you know what that is?"

Maggie thought there were a few possible answers.

"This," Roy said, pointing to his own head. "Our brain. The most powerful machine in the world. A dinosaur's brain is like a bird's. Really, it's about the same size. Compared to us a dinosaur is just like . . . a bird. I'm not going to let some kind of bird eat me, no matter how big it is. Are you?"

"Well, no, but . . ." Jacobs began.

"Exactly!" Roy said. "So I'm going. Who's with me?"

"This sounds exciting!" said Celia. "I'll go, too!"

"It's better than waiting," Dylan said.

"Maggie?" Roy said.

"Of course," said Maggie. Everyone turned to Jacobs.

"I think you're making a mistake," Jacobs began, "but as the only person from TimeTours it is my duty to . . ."

"Good," said Roy, hitting him on the back. "Let's go!"

Chapter 3

Dinosaur country

It wasn't long before they were lost. It began to rain, which made it hard to see as they pushed on through the jungle. Things were moving through the trees around them, and every once in a while there was a roar from somewhere. Maggie wished they were still at the storehouse, but after several hours it got a bit easier and they came to a river. They were up on a riverbank, high over the water. The river wasn't very wide, but getting down the wet riverbank looked difficult.

"Maybe we could go back?" she said to Roy, quietly.

"Which way?" he asked.

"Ah," Maggie replied. She had no idea where the storehouse was now. The others were looking at Roy, waiting for him to do something.

"What do you think, Mr. Jacobs?" Dylan asked him.

"I have no idea," said the TimeTours man. "I've never been this far from the Timeport."

"I think we need to get across the river," Roy said. "If we can get down and across it'll be easy to climb out." Climbing out may be easy, Maggie thought, but getting down would be hard. Nobody spoke.

"Are you sure that's the right way?" Dylan said. "Because I was looking at the map again and . . ."

"I'm going," Roy said.

"I think there's something moving around in the water," Jacobs said. "What do we do if it's a dinosaur?"

"'What if it's a dinosaur?'" Roy said in Jacobs's voice. He passed him his bag. "You just hold this."

Dylan started to take a rope out of his own bag.

"I've climbed Everest—twice," Roy said. "I think I can get down this riverbank."

"Please, Roy," Maggie said.

"Just to be safe," Dylan said "We'd be in real trouble without you." Maybe it was the light, but Maggie was sure he was smiling.

"OK, then," said Roy. He took the rope and put it around himself.

"Here," Dylan said, giving him a Boomer.

"If it'll make you all feel better . . ." Roy said, taking it.

Roy pushed the Boomer in his belt and started to go down the riverbank. Dylan held the other end of the rope.

"Be careful," Maggie said.

"Will you all stop worrying?" Roy told her. "This is a piece of ca . . . AAAAAH!" His foot slid on the wet riverbank and Roy began to slide down, the Boomer falling out of his belt and into the water with a splash. At the other end of the rope, Dylan started sliding toward the river.

"Hold on to me," Dylan shouted. Maggie ran forward and took the rope just before Dylan went over, but Roy was still falling. His arms and legs were moving like he was swimming, trying to find something to hold on to. He shouted in pain, then below him the water moved.

With a great roar, a big pair of jaws appeared. They belonged to a kind of crocodile, which Maggie thought was about the size of a bus, and it was trying to eat her husband.

"Help!" shouted Roy. "Help! Help!"

It seemed as though Roy was going to fall straight between its jaws. Jacobs, Maggie, and Dylan pulled hard on the rope, stopping his fall just before they went over themselves. Roy wasn't out of danger yet the crocodile was still trying to get him. Roy screamed and kicked at it.

"*Deinosuchus*," said Celia. "Wow. It must be 15 meters long."

"Will you hold this rope?" Maggie shouted. Celia took it and together they began to pull him up. It was difficult because Roy was moving around, trying to keep away from the dinosaur.

"Get me out of here," he shouted at them.

"Everyone: one, two, three, pull!" Dylan shouted. "Pull, pull, pull!" Roy was heavy but with the four of them pulling together they got him out of danger. But it took another minute of hard work to get him back up to the top of the bank, and by the end of it everyone was very tired.

"Th...thank you," Roy said.

"I guess we need to go another way," Dylan said.

Chapter 4

Positive thinking

An hour later they were on top of another hill, trying to decide where they were.

"I think we're here," Dylan said, showing everyone the map. "See the river? The main Timeport must be over there. I think we need to go this way." He pointed up the river.

"So we didn't need to go across the river after all," Jacobs said, looking at Roy.

"I don't think so," Dylan said. Roy opened his mouth to speak but then changed his mind. Instead he took Maggie's Boomer and started to play around with it. "Anyway, it's going to be dark soon," Dylan went on. "We should probably rest here for the night. Maybe we could try and make a fire."

"We must go back to the storehouse," Jacobs said.

"How are we going to do that?" Roy asked. "The TimeTours map doesn't even show where it is."

"Relax, everyone," Celia began. "Look around you. It may be millions of years ago but it's still the same Earth. We're still in the arms of Mother Nature. She's going to protect us, I know she will. Have any of you read *Positive Thinking*, by Anita Batty?" Everyone said no.

"That book changed my life," Celia went on. "It's just amazing. Batty teaches us that we can make anything happen if we strongly believe it. The way it works is you pick one thing, and say it over and over again and really believe it in a really positive way. So now I want us all to say 'Mother Nature will protect us' and really think it. Will you do that? I really think it would be great if we can all do that."

Celia looked at them all with wide eyes, waiting for an answer. Some time passed.

"Mother Nature will protect us," Maggie said, in the end.

"That's right!" said Celia. "Roy? Dylan?"

"Mother Nature will protect us," said Dylan.

"Sure, whatever," said Roy, then in a funny voice, "Mother Nature will protect us."

"Mr. Jacobs?" Celia went on. "Do you think you could say . . ."

"Mother Nature will protect us," Jacobs said. He said something else after it but Maggie couldn't hear what it was.

"You see?" Celia said. "Now I'm going to take all these great, positive thoughts and get us some food."

Celia went into the trees and Maggie and Dylan decided to look for some dry wood. Maggie made sure to stay close to Dylan and kept her Boomer in her hand. The roaring from the jungle seemed to be getting closer. To Maggie, it felt like something was going to jump out from the trees and attack them. By the time they had enough wood for a fire it was almost dark. They hurried back, but when they got there Celia was still out in the forest somewhere.

"One of us needs to look for her," Dylan said, dropping the wood on the ground. "You take care of the fire."

"That young woman has no idea of the danger," Jacobs was saying, walking back and forth. "It's all very well to talk about Mother Nature protecting us, but this is almost 70,000,000 years B.C. We were not even part of nature then."

"I know that, Jacobs," Roy said, "but that girl's walking about the forest in the dark. Aren't you going to do anything?"

"We can't just run after her and get ourselves killed," Jacobs said. "We need a plan."

"We need to find her, not sit around talking," Roy said. "Somebody help me up . . . aaargh, my leg."

"I'll go," Maggie said, although it was the last thing she wanted to do.

"Now wait a minute," said Roy.

"I'll go with you," said Dylan.

They were just about to go into the trees when they heard a voice behind them.

"Looking for me?" Celia asked. Her face was pink and she was smiling.

"Celia!" Maggie said. "We were worried about you!"

"You were out a very long time," Jacobs said. "Please be more careful."

"I told you, there was no need to worry," she said, taking off her pack and putting it on the ground. "Look what I got." She opened it and inside were things like bananas and some other kinds of fruit. "These are really good," she said, holding up something that looked like a big apple.

"Good girl," said Roy, taking it.

"Think positive thoughts and good things will happen," Celia began. "That's the secret, I think. Bad things happen only when you think about bad things. And I know lots of people have died and everything, but look at how beautiful everything is! Look at how amazing everything is! How can anything bad happen to . . . "

Before she could finish, there was a loud noise behind her. Celia started to turn, then flew back into the trees. She didn't even have time to scream.

"Something got her!" Dylan shouted. "Quick, make a circle!"

"But what *was* that?"

"Here," Jacobs said. In front of him stood the scariest thing Maggie could imagine. It stood about as tall as she did and had big, strong-looking claws. It wasn't just dangerous looking, Maggie thought. It was *intelligent* looking, too.

"Velociraptor," Jacobs said quietly, just as it jumped.

Chapter 5

Velociraptor!

It looked like the end for the TimeTours man. But before the dinosaur could reach him, Jacobs hit the switch on his Boomer and the dinosaur stopped. It gave a loud, angry cry and jumped back. Maggie pulled her own Boomer out of her bag and pushed the switch on it. The dinosaur cried out again.

"Here!" shouted Roy. Maggie turned. Two other Velociraptors came out from the trees. *It's their eyes,* Maggie thought. *They're full of intelligence, not like the eyes of birds at all.* "They're moving in groups," Roy added, still lying on the ground. "Make a circle! Not there— around me!"

One of them jumped forward toward Roy on the ground. Maggie felt sick with fear. She stepped in front of him holding the switch down on her Boomer with both hands. The dinosaur cried out again but began to back away slowly. The dinosaurs smelled very bad, like old meat.

"Turn it on and off," shouted Jacobs, "like this." He was pushing the switch, letting it go, then pushing it again. "They don't like that at all." Two more Velociraptors stood by the trees now, making five in all. They all were jumping this way and that, crying out with anger and pain.

"They won't be able to stand it much longer," Dylan said. As if in answer, one turned and ran back into the trees.

"You see?" Dylan said, smiling at Maggie. "We're winning!" Just as he said it, another Velociraptor jumped forward and hit him with its claw. The Boomer flew out of his hand.

"Dylan!" Maggie screamed. The Velociraptor's teeth closed on Dylan's arm, and then another dinosaur, seeing its chance, took him in its jaws.

"Get them off me!" Dylan shouted. "Help!"

Roy and Jacobs raced toward him, but it was too late. The Velociraptors pulled the young Australian into the trees. Maggie, Roy, and Jacobs stood alone around the fire as Dylan's screams grew quieter and then stopped.

"Man, that was bad," Roy said.

"Terrible," Jacobs was saying. "Terrible, terrible."

"Do you think he may be . . ." Maggie began. "You know, do you think maybe we could go in and . . ."

It was the first time Roy and Jacobs agreed on anything.

"No," they said together.

Jacobs got the fire started. Roy ate some of Celia's fruit but Maggie wasn't hungry, not after what happened. Instead she just listened to the jungle around them. Now and again there would be a roar or a cry from the trees, or what sounded like a scream, which made them all jump. It was going to be a long night. For the first time, Maggie started to think that she might not get back to their home in New York. *Don't say that, girl*, she thought to herself. *You have to be positive.* Then she found herself thinking about Celia, who showed, clearly, that positive thinking wasn't always enough.

Roy and Jacobs were arguing. Her husband was playing with one of the Boomers again and Jacobs wasn't too happy about it.

"Please put that down," Jacobs said. "What if you break it? Haven't enough bad things happened for one day?"

"That would be bad, wouldn't it?" Roy said. He held the Boomer above his head and brought it down hard on a rock.

"What are you doing?" Jacobs shouted.

"Roy?" said Maggie.

"Relax," said Roy, bringing it down a second time. The Boomer broke open.

"You . . . You . . ." Jacobs's face was red with anger. He was so angry he couldn't get the words out.

"Jacobs, please," Roy said. He was doing something inside the Boomer. "You may not know this, but before I started my own company and made trillions of dollars I was an engineer. I've built things 1,000 times more difficult than this. So just keep quiet and let me work."

Jacobs looked like he wanted to say something, but he just sat down and looked at the fire.

"There," Roy said. He put the Boomer back together and the power light went on. "Now you don't need to hold the switch down - it'll stay on all the time. And I've increased the power so it's *much* stronger. Nothing will come near us now."

"Is that a good idea?" Maggie said. "How much power does it have, Mr. Jacobs?"

"I'm not going to talk to this man anymore," Jacobs said.

"That's fine," Roy shouted. "Don't worry, Maggie. These things will work for thousands of hours. Isn't that right, Jacobs?"

"Well, yes, but . . ." Jacobs said.

"I thought you weren't talking to me?" Roy replied. Jacobs's face was red but he didn't say anything else.

"I'm real sorry about what happened to Dylan," Roy went on, "and that girl . . . what was her name again?"

"Celia," Maggie said.

"Now she had the right idea but she made one big mistake. Thinking positive isn't what's important. It's thinking smart. You hear what I'm saying? Thinking smart and doing smart. That's what puts us at the top— our brain." Roy pointed at the side of his head. "You all just wait and see. Tomorrow we're going to walk out of here, we're going to get to that Timeport, and by the evening we'll be back in Manhattan. Just you wait and see."

Chapter 6

The king of the jungle

When Maggie woke up it was light. She had no idea
when she fell asleep—she didn't think she *could* fall
asleep—but she was opening her eyes and it was
morning. Roy was happily eating a piece of fruit, but
the TimeTours man looked tired, as if he had stayed up
all night.

"I didn't sleep," he told Maggie. "Someone had to keep
watch."

"Have some fruit," Roy said to him.

Jacobs didn't reply to that.

"Come on," Roy said. Jacobs didn't reply. Roy stood up,
feeling his leg. "OK, Maggie's up, so let's go."

Maggie ate the last of the fruit, and the three of them set
off. Roy took the lead and Maggie was surprised to see
how well he was walking.

"How's your leg?" she asked. "Is it still hurting?"

"We haven't got time to worry about my leg," Roy said.
He's walking very easily, Maggie thought. *Was he really
hurt?* You never knew with Roy. Maggie found she was
more worried about Jacobs, who looked very tired.

"He's probably just worried about what'll happen when
he gets back. He'll probably lose his job for all this."

"But that's not fair," Maggie said.

"That's what happens."

If that was true, it really wasn't fair. She thought that Jacobs seemed like a good man. When they were safe she promised herself that she would thank him properly. And it seemed they would get back. With Roy's changes to the Boomer nothing came anywhere near them. Still, it was hot and Maggie often thought she would fall down, but just when she was sure she couldn't walk anymore, they came out of the forest. In front of them was a big open space with a lake in the middle. On the other side stood Timeport 11.

The sun was shining down on the water and on the far side were many big dinosaurs. Maggie knew the big Triceratops, but there were many others she didn't know. *They are so beautiful*, Maggie thought.

"Hey look," said Roy. "We're back on the big cow tour."

"I don't know how you can joke," Jacobs said, "after everything that's happened."

"Positive thinking, Jacobs," Roy said. "Positive thinking." He pointed at the Timeport. "There it is."

"I've never been out here before," Jacobs said. "Let's be careful."

"Let's be careful," Roy repeated, in Jacobs's voice.

Jacobs didn't answer and they started to make their way around the lake. Maggie was worried about Jacobs—he was getting more and more unhappy. She wanted Roy to leave him alone.

"Hey, Jacobs, a rescue party should be coming, right?" he was saying. "Oh, no, wait—this is TimeTours so maybe not."

Jacobs didn't speak.

"Look on the positive side," Roy went on. "You won't have to work for them much longer, because I'm going to put them out of business as soon as I get home. I'll take them for so much money . . ."

Maggie stopped suddenly and shouted, "Roy, will you, for once in your life, please, SHUT UP!?"

Roy turned and looked at her, surprised. She couldn't quite believe she said it herself. Roy looked like he wanted to say something but then there was a great sound from across the lake. The dinosaurs were all starting to move, fast, running for the trees. The noise was amazing.

"Did I just do that?" Maggie asked.

"I don't think so," said Jacobs. Suddenly, from out of the trees on the far side of the lake a very big and terrible dinosaur appeared. Maggie thought its head was bigger than her whole body.

"Is that . . . ? Is that . . . ?" Maggie began.

"A Tyrannosaurus Rex," Roy said. He was smiling.

Maggie and Jacobs watched with open mouths as the big dinosaur came around the edge of the lake. It caught one smaller dinosaur and ate it in one bite, hardly slowing down. It was coming toward them.

"Oh, man, will you just look at that?" Roy said. "The king of the jungle." He started walking toward it.

"That's not a good idea," Jacobs said.

"Roy, where are you going?" Maggie shouted.

"Put the camera on, Maggie," Roy said. "People are going to want to see this."

Maggie and Jacobs watched with their mouths open as Roy walked toward the big Tyrannosaur. For a moment it looked like it would run straight over him. Just before it reached him it stopped and roared.

"Oh, this?" Roy said, holding up the Boomer. "You don't like this? Hey, Maggie, are you getting this on camera?"

Maggie couldn't believe what she was seeing. She switched on the camera of her Com and turned it toward Roy and the Tyrannosaur.

"Who's the king of the jungle, now, huh?" Roy was saying. "Not so scary now you're . . ."

Roy stopped talking at that point because the power light on his Boomer went off. The Tyrannosaur roared and turned its head to the side, showing its teeth. It looked like it was smiling as it began to move toward Roy. Its jaws opened wide.

"Maggie! Help!" Roy screamed.

"We must do something," shouted Jacobs. He and Maggie both had Boomers; they had just enough time to throw one of them to Roy. The dinosaur had started to move faster; they had only a few seconds to save him.

"I'll throw him mine," Jacobs said.

"No!" shouted Maggie. "He's my husband. I'll do it!"

"Now!" shouted Roy. "Quick, Maggie, throw me the Boomer!"

Maggie only had one chance. If she missed, that was the end for Roy.

She held her breath, drew her arm back, and threw.

Chapter 7

Quiet

"You mustn't blame yourself, Mrs. Nagy," said Rose Whitson. The two women sat in a Timeport 11 office drinking coffee. Rose Whitson was the manager from TimeTours who organized their rescue. "It was all very difficult. Mr. Jacobs told me your throw was perfect. It really isn't your fault your husband dropped the Boomer in the lake. It must have been terrible. I'm so, so sorry. But you mustn't blame yourself. Really, you mustn't."

"I don't," said Maggie, drinking her cup of coffee. "I blame TimeTours."

"Of course, yes. Well, it was all very difficult," the woman went on. "I can't imagine how you're feeling, after all you've been through. If there is anything I can do, anything at all, please let me know."

A few times Maggie thought, *how about going back in time and saving everybody*? But that was one thing about traveling in time. You couldn't meet yourself—that was something nobody ever did—although Maggie wasn't sure why. Apart from that, Maggie didn't think there was anything anybody could do.

"I'm truly sorry about everything that's happened," Rose Whitson went on.

"Thank you," said Maggie.

"One last thing," said Rose Whitson. "May I ask if you

are . . . um . . . Do you think you may be planning to take action against TimeTours?"

"What kind of action?" Maggie asked her.

"The legal kind," said Rose Whitson. "I mean TimeTours would really like to keep everything quiet as much as possible."

"It depends," said Maggie. "I'd really like to go home now."

"Of course, yes," said Rose Whitson. "Thank you, Mrs. Nagy."

She got up and closed the door behind her, leaving Maggie alone in the office. She sat back and waited, hoping this time it wouldn't be too long.

They met the first TimeTours people only a few minutes after Roy died, and they brought Maggie and Mr. Jacobs back to safety. After that, the TimeTours people had a lot of questions. Every hour a new person wanted to ask her about what happened. Maggie didn't think there was anything else to tell by now. All morning she talked about the explosion, about making their way through the jungle and trying to get to Timeport 11. She told them about the computers not working at the storehouse and about what happened to Celia, Dylan, and, of course, Roy. She told them how she threw the Boomer to him, how he looked like he caught it, how it fell out of his hands and landed in the lake with a splash. Then how the Tyrannosaur . . . Thinking about it didn't feel real. One moment Roy was there, the next he wasn't. It felt like a dream, where everything was . . . she couldn't quite say what it was. She should be more upset, she knew, but right now it was hard to believe it all happened.

The door opened again. Maggie hoped it wasn't someone coming to ask her more questions. To her surprise it was Jacobs.

"Mr. Jacobs," Maggie said. "I wondered what happened to you."

"They've been asking me questions all afternoon," Jacobs said. "They told me to say you could go home now. Shall we?"

"Yes, please," Maggie said. She stood up and to her surprise Jacobs offered her his arm. She took it and he began to lead her through the building to the departure area.

"How are you feeling?" he said.

"Oh, you know," Maggie said. "Strange is the word for it. It all feels so strange. Without him."

"I'm very sorry about it all," Jacobs said. "I wish . . . Well, you know what I wish. I'm sorry about Roy, about everything."

"You did all you could," Maggie said. "Nobody can blame you. What did your company say?"

"I don't work for them anymore," Jacobs said.

"Oh no," Maggie said.

"It was my decision," Jacobs said rather proudly. "Your husband was right about this company. They are—now how did he say it?—'a joke.' I left."

They walked quietly for a while until they reached the departure area.

"What will you do now?" Jacobs asked.

"Go home and rest," Maggie told him.

"Then I'll have to take over all of Roy's things. The company is now mine, I suppose."

"I guess you'll be very busy."

"Yes, I guess so," she said. "You know, if you ever need some help, or if you are looking for another job, please let me know."

"Thank you," said Jacobs. "I'm sure I'll be fine, but it's nice of you to offer."

She said goodbye to Jacobs then as the other TimeTours people took her to the Timeship, so she could finally go back to 2738. Back home. She sat quietly in the Timeship and thought about what she would do back in the future. Now Roy was gone, his company and all his money would be hers, she supposed. She didn't have to manage it, she knew—she could sell it and never have to think about money again. Maybe she should take a little time to relax, she thought, settling back into her seat. Suddenly she knew what it was that felt so strange, so different from before.

It was quiet.

Review: Chapters 1–3

A. Read each statement and circle whether it is true (T) or false (F).

1. The story is about time travel into the future.   T / F

2. Coms are personal computers that all people carry with them.   T / F

3. TimeTours is a company specializing in time-travel tourism.   T / F

4. Roy is angry because TimeTours stole his money.   T / F

5. Dinosaurs don't like Boomers that are switched on.   T / F

B. Complete each sentence using the correct word from the box.

switch	equipment	brain	dangerous	smoke	fire

1. The tourists ran out of the building because the power room was on _____ .

2. Roy saw black _____ coming out of the door behind him.

3. Roy enjoyed walking through the jungle because he liked _____ things.

4. Inside the storehouse, they found food and _____ .

5. Roy pressed the power _____ on the big Com and a TimeTours woman came from the computer.

6. Roy is not afraid of dinosaurs because they don't have a human _____ .

C. Choose the correct answer in italics to complete the summary.

When Roy starts to slide down the **1.** (*hole* / *mountain* / *riverbank*), Dylan and Maggie stop him from falling by pulling back on the **2.** (*Boomer* / *rope* / *belt*). His weight makes them **3.** (*fall* / *slide* / *run*) toward the edge and for a moment it looks as though the big **4.** (*crocodile* / *Tyrannosaur* / *fish*) will eat him. Somehow they keep him out of its **5.** (*claws* / *arms* / *jaws*) and pull him back up to safety.

Review: Chapters 4–7

A. Match the characters in the story to their descriptions.

Maggie	Roy	Dylan	Celia	Mr. Jacobs

1. _____ is very positive about everything.
2. _____ is the best in the group at map-reading.
3. _____ doesn't like people saying bad things about his company.
4. _____ always thinks he's right.
5. _____ sometimes finds it difficult to be married.

B. Number these events in the order that they happened.

_____ But when Roy comes face to face with a big Tyrannosaur, all the power in his Boomer is gone.

_____ After Celia tells everybody about the importance of positive thinking, she is eaten by Velociraptors.

_____ Dylan is next to be eaten, and Maggie begins to think they may not get home.

_____ Only Maggie and Mr. Jacobs get home safely.

_____ As she's thinking about what might happen to them, Roy changes the power settings on his Boomer.

_____ Maggie tries to save him by throwing him her own Boomer, but Roy drops it in the lake and the Tyrannosaur gets him.

Answer Key

Chapters 1–3

A:
1. F; **2.** T; **3.** T; **4.** F; **5.** T
B:
1. fire; **2.** smoke; **3.** dangerous; **4.** equipment; **5.** switch; **6.** brain
C:
1. riverbank; **2.** rope; **3.** slide; **4.** crocodile; **5.** jaws

Chapters 4–7

A:
1. Celia; **2.** Dylan; **3.** Mr. Jacobs; **4.** Roy; **5.** Maggie
B:
4, 1, 2, 6, 3, 5

Background Reading:

Spotlight on . . . *Time Travel* . . .
Will it ever be possible?

Stories about time travel are very popular, and the idea of visiting the past or future is very exciting for most people. But will it ever be possible?

With today's scientific understanding, the answer is "maybe." Much of today's science is based on the work of Albert Einstein and his famous Theory of Relativity. In 1905, Einstein proved that time travel to the future is possible in theory because time moves more slowly at higher speeds.

The fastest thing in the universe is light. Light travels at about 300,000 km per second. For something traveling at this speed, time moves much more slowly than on Earth. If you travel for a few years at the speed of light, when you come back to Earth, you will be hundreds of years in the future. For example, if you travel 1,000 light years at almost the speed of light, time will slow down so much that you will only age ten years. But back on Earth, it will be 1,000 years later. In other words, a trip 1,000 years into the future could take ten years of flying close to the speed of light.

Will it ever be possible to fly at the speed of light? At the moment, nobody can say. The fastest ever flight with a human is a little less than 40,000 km per hour (the Apollo 10 capsule), so we have a long way to go!

And what about traveling to the past? That is a much more difficult question to answer, but to answer it, we might ask another question: if it is possible to visit the past, why hasn't anybody come back and visited us?

Think About It

1. Do you think time travel will ever be possible?

2. Where (or when) in time would you most like to go?

Glossary

claw	(*n.*)	people have nails at the end of their fingers, but animals have claws
engineer	(*n.*)	someone who works with and designs machinery
equipment	(*n.*)	things that you use for a particular task
joke	(*n.*)	something funny or not serious at all
jungle	(*n.*)	an area with lots of trees and wildlife
legal	(*adj.*)	related to the law
manage	(*v.*)	to control the operation of something, often a company
positive	(*adj.*)	good or helpful in some way
rescue	(*v.*)	to help someone get out of a bad situation
riverbank	(*n.*)	the land at either side of a river
roar	(*n.*)	a loud, angry cry
rope	(*n.*)	a long thin item, often used for climbing
scared/scary	(*adj.*)	when you think something bad is going to happen, and your heart beats faster, you are scared
slide	(*v.*)	to move smoothly, along ice or some kind of smooth ground
smoke	(*n.*)	the clouds of dust that come from a fire
storehouse	(*n.*)	a building where you keep things